My First Five Years

Images by
ANNE GEDDES

ANNE GEDDES ™

ISBN 1-55912-288-9

© Anne Geddes 1994

Published in 1997 by Photogenique Publishers (a division of Hodder Moa Beckett)
Studio 3.16, Axis Building, 1 Cleveland Road, Parnell
Auckland, New Zealand
First published in 1997 by Hodder Moa Beckett Publishers Limited

First published in 1997 by Cedco Publishing Company,
100 Pelican Way, San Rafael, CA 94901.

First USA edition 1997
Fifth printing, October 1997

Designed by Jane Seabrook
Produced by Kel Geddes
Color separations by MH Group
Printed through Colorcraft, Hong Kong

Please write to us for a FREE FULL COLOR catalog of our fine Anne Geddes
calendars and books, Cedco Publishing Company, 100 Pelican Way,
San Rafael, CA 94901.

Visit our website: www.cedco.com

ANNE GEDDES

*A*nne Geddes is an Australian-born photographer resident in Auckland, New Zealand. Her photographic studies have become extremely recognized and sought after in the American market in an ever increasing range of popular products.

My First Five Years remains one of Anne's best selling books, with her delightful and memorable images providing a perfect framework to display the joy and the keepsakes of those all too precious moments of birth and early childhood.

Anne says about her work, "To be able to capture on film the innocence, trust and happiness that is inherent in the next generation is a very special responsibility. It's work that rewards me daily with a great deal of personal satisfaction."

We know that the love, care and attention that will be detailed in this particular edition will be a source of enduring pride to be handed down from generation to generation.

Contents

My Birth

My Name is

_____

I was born on _____

at _____

The time was _____

I was delivered by _____

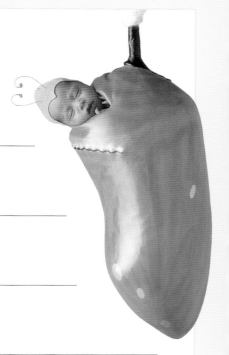

_____

I weighed

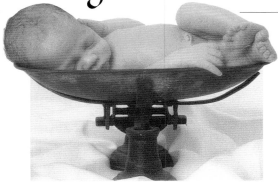

_____

and measured

_____

My eyes were _____

My hair was _____

7

Mementos

My Birth Announcement

A lock of hair

My hospital tag

Newspaper Clippings

What was happening in the world

Photographs

Comments

*Mother*_____

_____

_____

_____

*Father*_____

_____

_____

_____

Special Messages

Family

_____

_____

_____

_____

_____

Friends

_____

_____

_____

_____

Visitors and Gifts

_____

_____

_____

_____

_____

_____

_____

_____

_____

_____

Signs

Star Sign _____

_____

Chinese Year _____

_____

Birth Stone _____

_____

Birth Flower

Naming

My full name is _____

My name was chosen by _____

because _____

My pet names are _____

Ceremonies celebrating my birth _____

_____

Comments _____

_____

_____

_____

_____

Photographs

My Family Tree

Grandfather

(photo)

Grandfather

(photo)

Grandmother

(photo)

Grandmother

(photo)

Mother

(photo)

Father

(photo)

Baby

(photo)

I look like _____

_____

Photographs

Brothers and Sisters

Three Months

Weight _____

Length _____

Comments

_____

_____

_____

_____

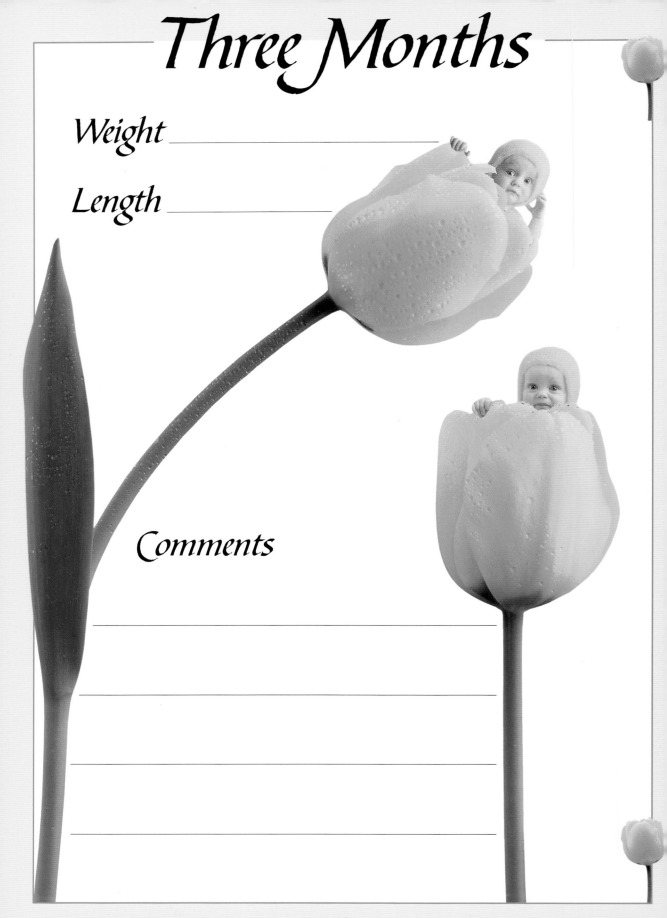

Photographs

Six Months

Weight _____   Length _____

Comments _____

_____

_____

_____

_____

Photographs

Nine Months

Weight _____

Length _____

Comments _____

_____

_____

_____

_____

_____

Photographs

Milestones

I first smiled _____

laughed _____

grasped a toy _____

I slept through the night

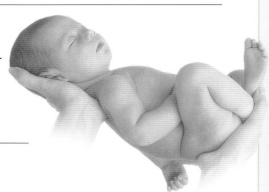

_____

I held my head up _____

rolled over _____

sat up _____

Comments _____

_____

_____

I first crawled _____

Stood up _____ walked _____

My first tooth _____

My first word _____

_____

Comments

_____

_____

_____

_____

Food

My first solid food _____

I was weaned _____

I drank from a cup _____

Finger food _____

I fed myself _____

I like _____

_____

_____

_____

_____

_____

I don't like _____

_____

_____

_____

My First Christmas

was at _____

Other people there

_____

_____

_____

My presents

_____

_____

_____

Photographs

My First Vacation

Was at _____

Date _____

The weather was _____

Other people there _____

_____

_____

Comments

_____

_____

Photographs

My First Birthday

I live at _____

_____

My height is _____

Weight _____

Sayings _____

_____

Toys _____

Pets _____

Books _____

_____

My Party

Date _____

Where held _____

Friends and relations there _____

_____

_____

_____

My presents _____

_____

_____

_____

Photographs

Clothes

The first time I dressed myself

_____

I wore _____

My favorite dress-ups

_____

_____

I won't wear

_____

Comments _____

_____

Photographs

Favorites

Music _____

_____

_____

_____

Rhymes _____

_____

Clothes _____

_____

Animals _____

_____

*Activities*_____

_____

_____

Television Programs _____

_____

_____

_____

I really don't like _____

_____

_____

_____

Best Friends

One Year

photo

Two Years

photo

Comments

_____

_____

_____

Three Years

photo

Comments

_____

_____

_____

_____

_____

Four Years
photo

Five Years
photo

_____

_____

_____

_____

My Second Birthday

I live at _____

My height is _____ Weight _____

Sayings _____

Toys _____

_____

Pets _____

_____

Books _____

_____

_____

My Party

Date _____

Where held _____

Friends and relations there

_____

_____

_____

_____

My presents _____

_____

_____

_____

Photographs

My Third Birthday

I live at _____

My height is _____ Weight _____

Sayings _____

_____

Toys _____

Pets _____

Books _____

_____

_____

_____

My Party

Date _____

Where held _____

Friends and relations there _____

_____

_____

_____

_____

My presents

_____

_____

Photographs

My Fourth Birthday

I live at _____

_____

My height is _____

Weight _____

Sayings _____

_____

_____

Toys _____

Pets _____

Books _____

My Party

Date _____

Where held _____

Friends and relations there _____

_____

_____

_____

My presents _____

_____

_____

_____

Photographs

Pre-School

*My first day at pre-school was on*_____

_____ *at* _____

My teacher is _____

Comments _____

A _____

_____

_____

B _____

_____

C D E F

Photographs

G  H  I J

My Fifth Birthday

I live at _____

My height is _____ *Weight* _____

Sayings _____

Toys _____

_____

Pets _____

_____

Books _____

_____

_____

My Party

Date _____

Where held _____

_____

Friends and relations there

_____

_____

_____

My presents _____

_____

_____

_____

Photographs

Kindergarten

I started on _____

at _____

My friends are _____

_____

Comments _____

_____

_____

_____

_____

Photographs

Drawings

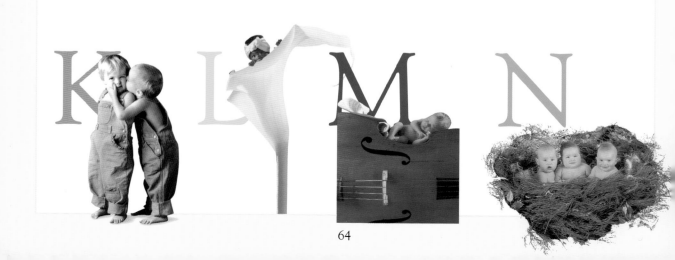

K L M N

O *h no!*

P

Q

R

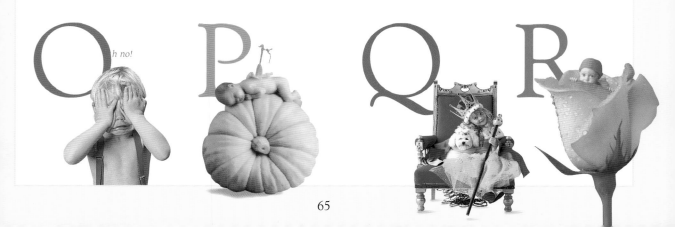

Writing

I could recite the alphabet _____

_____

I started to write _____

I began to read _____

My writing _____

_____

_____

_____

_____

W X Y Z

Health

Immunization

Age	Vaccine	Date given

Allergies

_____

_____

_____

Illnesses _____

_____

_____

Comments _____

_____

_____

_____

My Height

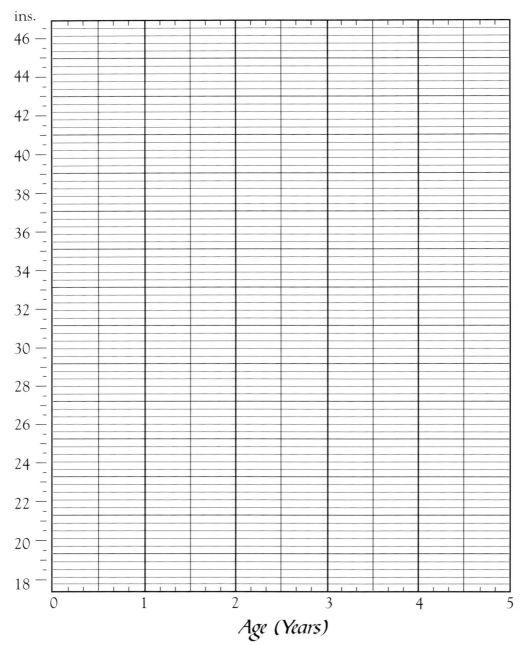

ins.

Age (Years)

My Weight

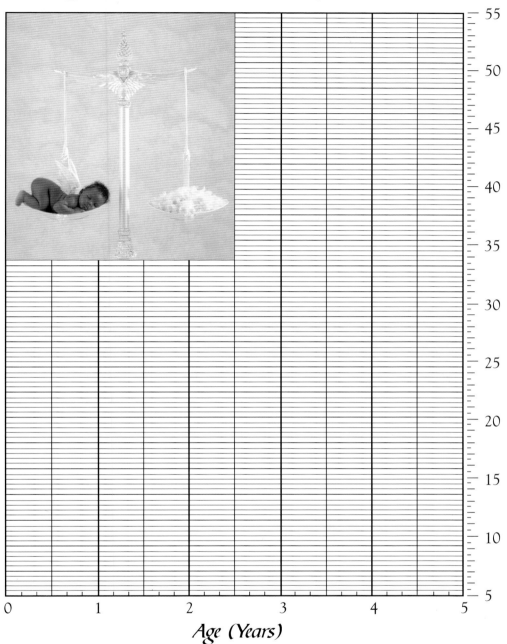

lb

55

50

45

40

35

30

25

20

15

10

5

0   1   2   3   4   5

Age (Years)

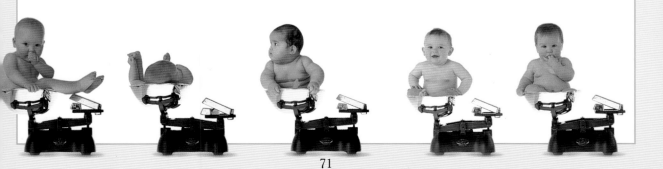

My Teeth

Upper Jaw

Date

8
9
16
13
24

Months

24
13
16
10
7

Date

Lower Jaw

Visits to the dentist

72

The Tooth Fairy's page

I lost my first tooth on _____

My second tooth _____

The Tooth Fairy left me _____

_____

Comments _____

_____

_____

_____

_____

My Handprints

At birth

At five years

My Footprints

At birth

At five years

Star Signs

Capricorn
22 December – 20 January
Resourceful, self-sufficient, responsible

Aquarius
21 January – 18 February
Great caring for others, very emotional
under cool exterior

Pisces
19 February – 19 March
Imaginative, sympathetic, tolerant

Aries
20 March – 20 April
Brave, courageous, energetic, loyal

Taurus
21 April – 21 May
Sensible, love peace and stability

Gemini
22 May – 21 June
Unpredictable, lively, charming, witty

Cancer
22 June – 22 July
Love security, comfort

Leo
23 July – 23 August
Idealistic, romantic, honorable, loyal

Virgo
24 August – 23 September
Shy, sensitive, value knowledge

Libra
24 September – 23 October
Diplomat, full of charm and style

Scorpio
24 October – 22 November
Compassionate, proud, determined

Sagittarius
23 November – 21 December
Bold, impulsive, seek adventure

Birth Stones

January	Garnet – Constancy and truth
February	Amethyst – Sincerity, humility
March	Aquamarine – Courage and energy
April	Diamond – Innocence, success
May	Emerald – Tranquillity
June	Pearl – Precious, pristine
July	Ruby – Carefree, chaste
August	Moonstone – Joy
September	Sapphire – Hope, chastity
October	Opal – Reflects every mood
November	Topaz – Fidelity, loyalty
December	Turquoise – Love and success

Flowers

January	Snowdrop – Pure and gentle
February	Carnation – Bold and brave
March	Violet – Modest
April	Lily – Virtuous
May	Hawthorn – Bright and hopeful
June	Rose – Beautiful
July	Daisy – Wide-eyed and innocent
August	Poppy – Peaceful
September	Morning Glory – Easily contented
October	Cosmos – Ambitious
November	Chrysanthemum – Sassy and cheerful
December	Holly – Full of foresight

Comments

Photographs

Comments _____

_____

_____

_____

_____

_____

_____

_____

_____

Photographs